Gems from THE UPANISHADS

Gems from THE UPANISHADS

H.P. PHILLIPS

Sri Ramakrishna Math
MYLAPORE, CHENNAI – 600 004

Published by :
The President
Sri Ramakrishna Math
Mylapore, Chennai - 4

VII-2M 3C-1-2005
ISBN 81-7120-935-1

Printed in India at
Sri Ramakrishna Math Printing Press
Mylapore, Chennai - 4

Preface

We have great pleasure in presenting to our readers this pretty "Garland of Gems from the Upanisads."

Aptly have the Upanisads been named the Himalayas of the Soul. *Puruṣāt na param kiñcit*: There is no limit to the heights to which the human spirit can soar. And the Upaniṣads are the expressions of some of the finest moments of the experiences of our ancient sages in their contemplation of the Divine. We do not know how many millennia have passed since those inspired talks were recorded in our forest universities. But age has not withered nor custom staled their unfading freshness and charm. It must however be borne in mind that these utterances form not so much a logical approach to Reality as a poetic apprehension of It. Hence we can find in them philosophic concepts at different levels. As Sri Ramakrishna has observed from the profundity of his own experience, the aspirant has to choose from them what suits best his particular mental and emotional make up.

Prof. H.B. Phillips who has, as a labour of love, selected 108 gems from the Upaniṣadic mine and strung them into a fascinating array, is a Sanskrit scholar from S. Africa. He is intensely interested in Indian scriptures and holds the certificate of *Vedācārya.* We are grateful to him not only for compiling this brief anthology but also for partly subsidizing its publication.

Publisher

Sri Ramakrishna Math,
Chennai
September 1977

A Garland of Gems from The Vedic Upanishads

Table of Contents

PART - I

Dualism

PART - II

Qualified Non-dualism

PART - III

Non-dualism

Introduction to the Upanishads

THE word Upaniṣad[1], whatever its original meaning, soon came to signify "secret or esoteric doctrine," as in Śvetāśvatara 5.6: "That which is hidden in the secret of the Vedas, even the Mystic Doctrines (Upaniṣad)" (Hume). As the earliest Upaniṣads generally came at the end of the Brāhmaṇas and or Āraṇyakas, themselves a late stage in Vedic literature, they are also referred to as Vedānta or "end of the Veda". The great commentator, Sankara, wrote commentaries on most of these, together with a few others, eleven in all, and these are the ones chosen for selection in this work. Altogether there are over 200 so called Upaniṣads, although the tradit˙onal number is fixed at 108. Some of these teach Vedānta, but most are more concerned with Yoga, Sannyāsa, or glorifying Viṣṇu, Śiva, Śakti, etc., and so can make

1. The Meaning that Śankara gives to the word is 'that which shatters ignorance'. While etymologically the word has also got the meaning given by the author, 'secrecy' associated with it is not meant to hide anything unseemly from view. High moral and spiritual qualifications are required to understand the true import of the Upaniṣads, and so the ancients taught them only to a restricted circle of highly qualified disciples.

—*Publishers*

no serious claim to belong to the Vedic cycle. To date the early Upaniṣads is difficult, even to arrange them in sequence, but it is generally agreed, I think, that the longer prose Upaniṣads belong to 8th and 7th centuries B.C. and are pre-Buddhistic. Some of the later of these "Vedic" Upaniṣads, like Śvetāśvatara refer to Yoga and perhaps Śiva.

In his *History of Sanskrit Literature,* A.A. Macdonell claims that the Upaniṣads represent a new religion (p.220), and certainly M. Winternitz *(A History of Indian Literature,* Vol. I Part I, 3rd Ed. p.198ff) points out that their teachings were against the plurality of gods and were rather connected with the warrior-caste and others than with the priests. I think that at least Macdonell goes too far: "Seers had a direct intuitive insight into duty. They by oral instruction handed down the hymns (he is referring here to the Saṁhitas) to later generations who were destitute of the direct intuitive insight. The later generations, declining in the power of oral communication, compiled this work in order to comprehend their meaning" (Yaska's Nirukta 1.20, Tr. Sarup). We might add that the Upaniṣads were similarly direct intuitive insights. At any rate they are "vehicles more of spiritual illumination than of systematic reflection; their aim is practical rather than speculative" *(A Source Book in Indian Phillosophy,* Radhakrishnan and Moore, ad loc.) That they are in the direct line of Rigvedic inspiration is shown by the following parallelisms:

Upaniṣadic Gem	*Doctrine*	*Vedic Parallel*
3	Three Strands	AV.10.8.43
25	Two birds	RV.1.164.20
26	The Gāyatri	RV.3.62,10
31	Pattern corresponding to every form	RV.6.47.18
32	World tree	RV.1.24.7
34–35	Unity of the gods	RV.2.1.3–4
42	He who eats alone	RV.10.117.6
44–45	Gods and Ancestors	RV.10.14.3 & 15.2
48–50	Rebirth	RV.1.164.30,38
56	One, and three quarters	RV.10.90.3–4
58ff	Paradoxes	RV.I.164.30
64	Plate hides Truth	YV.40.17
62	Māyā	RV.6.47.18
65	Māyā	RV.10.177.1
66	Prajāpati the First–born	AV.10.8.13 & YV.32.4
67	Facing all ways	YV.17.19
68	Thousand–headed	RV.10.90.1
69	Man and woman	AV.10.8.27
75	Immortal Self	RV.I.164. 30,38
77–78	Light in heart	YV.32. 8–9 RV.6.9.4–5
78	Light of lights	YV.34.1
	The Sun not there	RV.9.113.9–10
94	Grace	RV.10.71.4 RV.10.125.5

Upaniṣadic Gem	*Doctrine*	*Vedic Parallel*
86, 88	Searching for the Self	RV.1.65.1; 72.2 RV.10.46.2
103	Holes bored in head	AV.10.2.6; 11.8.18
107	Morning Light	RV.8.6.30
	Highest Light	RV.1.1.10
108	Realisation	YV.31.18
Bṛhad.3.7.1,2,7	Thread of Thread	AV.10.8.38

According to Radhakrishnan and Moore (op.cit.). the Upaniṣads are concerned with the search for the Reality underlying the Flux of things—One God of whom the Vedic gods are manifestations. This Real, which is at the heart of the universe (Brahman), is reflected in the infinite depths of the Self (Ātman). But this Supreme cannot be defined by logical categories. It is the incomprehensible Nirguṇa or Qualityless Brahman, but It is envisaged as Saguṇa (Qualified) Brahman or Īśvara (Lord, Personal God), when It is viewed as the constitutive Reality of the Many or the Cause of the world, as the Ground of the selves. The Upaniṣads speak to us of the way in which thẹ indiviual self gets at the Ultimate Reality by an inward journey, an inner ascent. This requires adequate moral preparation, and the goal is identity with the supreme.

Where the text is prose, I have translated in prose; where it is verse, I have used verse, aiming at reproducing the metre as far as possible—not syllable by syllable, but along broad lines. I have arranged my selection under headings in an attempt to systematise the thought of the Upaniṣads without the need for commentary, but I am aware that I may not always have correctly identified the category to which certain texts belong—Dvaita, Viśiṣṭhādvaita or Advaita; or whether the Brahman referred to is Transcendent, Immanent or Individual. But after all, that is one of the beauties of Vedantic thought—it allows a certain latitude of interpretation, otherwise how could there be the different schools of thought!

—H.B. Phillips

*The Master accepted
all the doctrines
of Non-dualism (Advaita),
Qualified Non-dualism
(Visishtadvaita) and Dualism
(Dvaita). But he used to say:
"These three doctrines are
accepted by the human mind
according to the stage
of its progress."*

*(Sri Ramakrishna, the Great Master,
3rd Edition, p. 388)*

Part - I

Dualism or the Worldly Life

MATTER AND SPIRIT

1. Verily the Lord of Creation was desirous of progeny; he underwent religious austerity. Having undergone austerity, he produced a pair—Matter and Life, thinking, "These two will produce progeny for me in many ways."

Verily the sun is Life, and Matter is the Moon; Matter verily is everything here, both what has form and the formless; therefore form is Matter.

—*Praśna 1.4-5*

2. Two unborn there are, one unknowing, t'other
wise, and thirdly Nature provides enjoyment.
Universal, endless, inactive that Soul
which beholds this triad as one with Brahman.

—*Śvetāśvatara 1.9*

MATTER OR NATURE

3. Red and white and black is that Goat called Nature,
bearing many offspring, each like the mother
One he-goat there is which takes his delight beside her,
t'other takes his pleasure and disgusted leaves her. *—Śvet.4.5*

4. That Being thought: "Would that I were many; let me procreate myself." It projected Fire. That Fire thought: "Would that I were many; let me procreate myself." It projected Water.

That Water thought: "Would that I were many; let me procreate myself." It projected Food *(=Earth).* *—Chāndogya 6.2.3-4*

5. In gross fire that colour which is red is the colour of subtle fire, that which is white belongs to water, that which is black to food (earth).

—Chāndogya 6.4.1

6. Food when eaten becomes divided into three parts: its coarsest ingredient becomes faeces; the middling becomes flesh; the finest becomes mind.

Water when drunk becomes divided into three parts: Its coarsest ingredient becomes urine; the middling becomes blood; the finest becomes vital force.

Fire (in the form of oil, fat, etc.) when eaten becomes divided into three parts: Its coarsest ingredient becomes bone; the middling becomes marrow; the finest becomes voice.

Hence, my dear, the mind consists of food, the vital force consists of water, the voice consists of fire. — *Chāndogya 6.5.1-4*

(Note: These references to three elements do not imply that there was a three-element stage in Indian thought: they are merely the more obvious of the five elements.)

7. He said to them: "Enter each into his abode."
Fire having become the voice entered the mouth;
Air having become breath entered the nostrils;
the sun having become sight entered the eyes;
the Quarters having become hearing entered the ears;
Plants and Trees having become hairs entered the skin;
the moon having become the mind entered the heart;..
Water having become semen entered the generative organ.

—*Aitareya 1.2.4*

8. From this Self verily Ether arose,
from Ether Air, from Air Fire,
from Fire Water, from Water Earth,

from Earth Plants, from plants
food, and from food the person arose.

—*Taittirīya 2.1.3*

9. He is Brahma, He is Indra, He is the Lord of Creation, He is all the gods, and the five Great Elements; Earth, Air, Ether, Water, Fire.

—*Aitareya 3.5.3*

SPIRIT

(a) The Gods

10. For fear of Brahman Fire gives heat,
for fear of Him the Sun shines strong,
For fear both Indra and the Wind
with Death as fifth all speed along.

—*Kaṭha 6.3*

11. That by which these sounds[1] are heard,
not that which one can hear by ear,
That alone as Brahman know,
not this which people worship here.

—*Kena 1.7*

(b) Souls

1. THE FIVE SHEATHS

2. ....Verily this Person consists of the essences of food.

---

1. Lit. hearing.

"From food all creatures are produced,
as many as on earth are found;
By food they live and food become
at last, when buried in the ground."

There is another Self than this one consisting of the essence of Food—the one consisting of Vital Energy. This is filled by that

"God and men and animals
must needs all breathe this Vital force,
Therefore the life it is of all;
of all they say it is the source."

There is another Self than this one consisting of Vital Energy—the one consisting of Mind. This is filled by that....

....Verily there is another Self than this one consisting of Mind—the one consisting of Intelligence. This is filled by that....

There is another Self than the one consisting of intelligence the one consisting of Bliss. This is filled by that.... —*Taittirīya 2.1-5*

2. THE WAKING STATE

13. Which is the self? That which consists of Intelligence, which is amid the organs, which is the light

---

1. Head, right and left eyes, breath, body, lower organ, feet, cp. Chāndogya 5.18.2.)

2. Five sense-organs, five organs of action, five vital breaths, and the four aspects of the internal organ, namely, sensorium, intellect, ego, and mind-stuff.)

within the heart. Remaining the same, it traverses both worlds; it appears to think, it appears to move to and fro. —*Bṛhad.4.3.7*

14. The waking state, outwardly cognitive, seven-limbed[1], nineteen-mouthed[2], experiencing gross objects-such is the first quarter common to all men. —*Māṇḍūkya 3*

3. THE DREAM STATE

15. Verily there are only two conditions of this Person—this life and that in the other world; the dream-state at the junction of the two is a third. Taking its stand at the junction, it sees both these conditions this life and that in the other world... When it dreams, taking away a little of this all-embracing world, making itself insensible, it constructs for itself a dream body, and dreams by its own brightness, by its own light.....

In that state there are no chariots, no teams, no roads, but it projects chariots, teams and roads;

In that state there are no joys, no pleasures, no delights, but it projects joys, pleasures and delights; in that state there are no tanks, pools or rivers, but it projects tanks, pools and rivers; for it is a creator.

"When dreaming, the mind, many roles assuming,
Some higher, some lower, creates its objects;

With women he seems to be making merry,
or laughing perhaps, or beholding dangers."

—*Bṛhad. 4.3.9,10,13*

16. The dream state, inwardly cognitive, seven-limbed, nineteen mouthed, experiencing subtle objects—such is the second quarter consisting of Light.

—*Māṇḍūkya 4*

4. DEEP SLEEP

17. Just as a hawk or an eagle flying about in the sky becomes weary, and folding its wings is borne down to its nest, even so this Person hastens to the state where falling asleep he desires no object, sees no dream.

Indeed, this is that form of his which is beyond desires, is bereft of evil, is free from fear. Just as a man closely embraced by his dear wife knows nothing within or without, even so this Person closely embraced by the Intelligent Self knows nothing within or without; indeed, that is his true form in which all objects of desire have been satisfied, in which they have become the Self, which is desireless, free from sorrow.

In this state a father is no more a father, a mother no more a mother, people no more people, the gods no more gods, the Vedas no more Vedas.....

"He becomes an ocean, the one seer, free from duality; this is the world that is Brahman, O king!"

thus Yājnavalkya instructed him. "This is his highest goal...... this is his highest bliss."

—*Bṛhad.4.3.19,21,22,32*

18. That is deep sleep where the sleeper desires no object, sees no dream. The state of deep sleep is with experiences all unified, with cognition reduced to a mere indefinite mass, consisting of bliss, enjoying bliss, forming the gateway to definite cognitions such is the third quarter, the Intellectual. —*Māṇḍukya 5*

19. Just as those who do not know their field might walk over a hidden treasure of gold again and again and not find it, even so all creatures here daily go into the world of Brahman in deep sleep, but do not find IT, for they are enveloped by falsehood. —*Chāndogya 8.3.2*

5. DEATH

20. When this Self comes to weakness and to insensibility, as it were, then those organs gather around him; taking to himself those particles of energy, he descends into the heart; when this Person that is in the eye turns back on all sides, then he becomes unable to distinguish colours.... the upper end of his heart lights up; by that light this Self departs—either through the eye, or the head, or other parts of the body; the vital force accompanies him as he goes out; all the organs

accompany the vital force when it goes out; he becomes fused with Intelligence; he descends into what is fused with Intelligence. His meditation, the results of his actions, and his previous impressions follow him. —*Bṛhad.4.4.1-2*

21. My dear, his relatives sit around a man who is ill, asking, "Do you know me? Do you know me?" As long as his voice does not enter into his mind, his mind into his breath, his breath into his body-heat, his body-heat into the highest divinity, so long does he know.

But when his voice is absorbed into his mind, his mind into his breath, his breath into his body-heat, his body-heat into highest divinity, then he knows not. —*Chāndogya 6.15.1-2*

THE LIFE OF IGNORANCE

22. Therefore even now people in this world say of one who does not give, who does not believe, who does not sacrifice, "Oh, he is a devil!" For such is the secret-doctrine of devils. —*Chāndogya 8.8.5*

23. Abiding in ignorance deeply sunken,
    self-wise they consider themselves as learned.
They wander about, running round deluded,
    the blind as if led by a blind man blindly.
A life after death is not clear to the childish,
    indifferent, by love of money deluded.

1. Death is speaking.

"The world's here alone, no place other," thinking,
again and again him I get in my[1] power.
—Kaṭha 2.5-6

24. The foolish pursue pleasures outward-facing:
they walk to be caught in Death's snare
wide-gaping.
The wise having tasted of life immortal
here seek not th'Eternal among the transient.
—Kaṭha 4.2

PART - II

Qualified Non-dualism
or
The Religious Life

THE PERSONAL GOD, THE LORD

25. Two fine birds united in kinship, comrades,
occupy a tree as their common dwelling.
One of these is eating the peepul-berries,
t'other looks on silently, never eating.
On this tree the person, in worldliness sunken,
aware of his impotence, grieves, bewildered.
But when he beholds the adored other—
the Lord and His glory—his sorrow ceases.

—*Muṇḍaka 3.1.1-2*

26. The dark is dispelled, no night nor daylight,
nor Being nor Void, but the kindly one[1] solely,
Immutable He, the "Sun's choicest splendour;"[1]
from Him has proceeded the Ancient Wisdom.

—*Śvetāśvatara 4.18*

THE RELATIONSHIP OF SOULS TO THE LORD

27. Just as a spider voids its body by a thread, just as tiny sparks go forth from a fire, even so from this Self all the organs, all the worlds, all the gods, all things go forth.

—*Bṛhad.2.1.20*

28. As its web a spider emits and draws in,
just as plants arise on the earth and wither,
Just as hair develops on living persons,
even so this world from the Self arises.

—*Muṇḍaka.1.1.7*

29. This here is the truth:
Often we may see from a blazing furnace
hot and ruddy sparks by the thousand flying;
Even so, my boy, from the Self emerging,
rise and set at last many diverse creatures.

—*Muṇḍaka 2.2.1*

---

1. Siva.
2. A quotation from the Gayatri Prayer.

THE FIGURE OF THE CHARIOT

30. Know that the Self is the master,
the body is the car, 'tis plain;
Know the intellect as the driver,
and the mind of course the rein.
The senses are the horses, sure,
the objects, roads that here, there wind;
The wise him call the enjoyer
combined with body, sense and mind.

—*Kaṭha 3.3-4*

THE RELATIONSHIP OF THE WORLD TO THE LORD

(a) The Figure of Fire

31. Just as the one fire, the world having entered,
becomes corresponding to ev'ry object,
Just so the one Self of all things existing
appears with like form, and is outside also.

—*Kaṭha 5.9*

(b) The Figure of the World-Tree

32. Its roots above, its branches down,
this is the eternal Peepul-tree.
That is the Brahman, that the light.
that they call Immortality.

On it rest all the worlds supported,
nothing beyond it wanders free.
This verily is That.

—Kaṭha 6.1

(c) The Mystery of Tajjalān

33. Verily everything here is Brahman: He is That (ta) from which all things originate (ja); That which sustains all things (an); That into which all things will be dissolved (la) so one should meditate in tranquillity.

—Chāndogya 3.14.1

THE RELATIONSHIP OF THE GODS TO THE LORD

34. He burns as fire, shines as the sun,
Falls as bountiful rain, blows as the wind;
Matter He, and earth, and god,
both false and true
is He, immortal too.[1]

—Praśna 2.5

35. That is Air, the moon is That.
That same is Fire and also Sun.

---

1. The text is printed as poetry, but the metre is uncertain.

That is Brahman, Light and Water
and Creator - all in One.

—*Svetāśvatara 4.2*

THE ETHICAL LIFE – SUNDRY MAXIMS

36. Having taught the Veda, the teacher directs his pupil thus: Speak the truth. Practise virtue. Do not neglect the study of the scriptures. Offer an acceptable gift to the teacher, and do not cut off the line of your progeny. You must not be negligent of the truth. You must not be negligent of virtue. You must not be negligent of your well-being. You must not be negligent of prosperity. You must not be negligent of studying and teaching the scriptures.

You must not be negligent of the rites owing to the gods and the Ancestors. Worship your mother. Worship your father. Worship your teacher. Worship the guest. Whatever acts are irreproachable, those you must do, and no others. Whatever deeds among us are good deeds, those you must perform, and no others. Whoever are Brahmins superior to us, you must make them comfortable with a seat. Give willingly. Do not give unwillingly. Give according to your resources. Give with modesty. Give with fear.[1] Give with sympathy.

—*Taittirīya 1.11. 1-3*

1. "There but for the grace of God go I!"

37. The three kinds of sons of Prajāpati lived with their father Prajāpati studying the Veda–gods, men and demons. Having finished study of the Veda, the gods said, "Let your Honour speak to us." To them he spoke this syllable, "Da. Do you understand?" "we understand", they said. "You said, 'Control yourselves (dāmyata).' " "Yes," he answered, "you understand."

Then the men said to him, "Let your Honour speak to us." To them he spoke this syllable, "Da, Do you understand?" "We understand," they said, "You said, 'Be charitable (datta)!' " "Yes," he answered, "you understand."

Then the demons said to him, "Let your Honour speak to us." To them he spoke this syllable, "Da. Do you understand?" "We understand," they said. "You said, Be compassionate (dayadhvam).' " "Yes," he answered, "you understand." Therefore this divine voice, the thunder, repeats this same syllable, "Da Da Da—Control yourselves, Be charitable, Be compassionate," Therefore one should learn this triad of—self-control, charity, compassion.

—Bṛhad. 5.2. 1-3

38. Verily, he speaks surpassingly who speaks surpassingly with truth.

—Chāndogya 7.16

---

1. Dharma.

39. Verily when one thinks, then one understands. Without thinking one does not uderstand, but after having thought one understands.

—*Chāndogya 7.18*

40. ......There is nothing higher than the Right[1]; so a weaker man hopes to overcome the stronger by means of what is Right, just as by a king. Verily that which is right is truth, therefore they say of a speaker of truth that he speaks rightly, or of a speaker of the Right that he speaks truly. Verily they are both the same thing.

—*Bṛhaḍ.1.4. 14*

41. One should not run down food. That is a rule. Life indeed is food.

—*Taittirīya 3.7.*

42. One should not refuse anyone at one's dwelling. That is a rule. Therefore one should acquire much food by any means whatever. Of such a one, people say, "Food is prepared for the sake of the guest."

Verily this food that has been prepared for the guest first, this food prospers for him (viz. the host) first; this food verily which has been prepared for the guest in the middle, this food prospers for the host in the middle; this food verily which has been prepared for the guest last, this food prospers for the host last—for him who knows thus.

—*Taittirīya 3.10*

43. One thing is the good, another the pleasant;
they both bind a man though with aims divergent.
'Tis well for the one who the better chooses;
he fails of his aim who prefers the pleasant.

—Kaṭha 2. 1

REINCARNATION

(a) The Two Paths and Five Fires

44. Now indeed there are three worlds—the world of men, the world of the Ancestors, the world of the gods. This world of men here is to be gained only by a son and by no other means, the world of the Ancestors by rites, the world of the gods by meditation. The world of the gods verily is the best of the worlds, therefore they praise meditation.

—Bṛhad. 1.5.16

45. Those who in the forest consider faith as austerity pass into the flame of the pyre, from the flame into the day, from the day into the half-month of the waxing moon, from the half month of the waxing moon into those six months during which the sun shifts northwards; from those months into the year, from the year into the sun, from the sun into the moon, from moon into the lightning; there a non-human person leads them to Brahman. This is the path leading to the gods.

Those who in the village honour sacrifice and pious works and alms-giving pass into the smoke of the pyre, from the smoke into the night, from the night into the latter half of the month, from the latter half of the month into the six months during which the sun shifts southwards, but they do not reach the year.

From those months they pass into the world of the Ancestors, from the world of the Ancestors into space, from space into the moon...

Residing in that region as long as there is a residue of merit, they then return again by the same path as they came into space, from space into the wind; having become wind they turn into vapour, having become vapour they turn into mist. Having become mist they turn into a rain-cloud, having become a rain-cloud they fall as rain. They are born again in this world as rice or barely, as plants or trees, as sesame or beans; from these indeed escape is difficult. Only if someone eats them as food, and emits them as semen, do they become just like him.

Whoever in this world are of pleasant conduct, the prospect is that they enter a pleasant womb like that of a Brahmin, a Kshatriya, or a Vaisya; but those who in this world are of stinking conduct, the prospect is that they enter a stinking womb like that of a dog, a swine, or an outcast.

But by neither of these two paths go the small repeatedly-returning creatures of whom it is said, "Be born and die". That is a third state.

—*Chāndogya 5.10.1-8*

46. In ignorance live diversely the childish;
 they think of themselves as their aim accomplished.
 Therefore the wretches, their heaven expended,
 sink down from desire in absence of knowledge.

—*Muṇḍaka 1.2.9*

47. From Him is produced the heavens above us,
 thence rain from the moon, and the plants here growing;
 From food grows the semen the male discharges,
 thus numberless creatures arise by Nature.

—*Muṇḍaka 2.1.5*

(b) Rebirth determined by one's desires

48. The man with desires who keeps brooding on them
 because of desires has rebirths repeated.
 The goal if attained and himself perfected,
 desires of themselves all vanish completely.

—*Muṇḍaka 3.2.2*

(c) Karma

49. Just as an embroiderer, taking off the loom a piece of embroidered cloth, weaves another newer and

more beautiful form, so this Self, setting aside this body, causing it to become insensible, creates another newer and more beautiful form.

According to one's actions, according to one's conduct, so one becomes—the doer of good becomes good, the doer of evil becomes evil; a man becomes virtuous by virtuous action, sinful by sin.

Now they say further that this Person is made up of desires alone; as he desires so he resolves, as he resolves so he acts, as he acts so he becomes.

—Bṛhad. 4.4. 4-6

50. Some enter in a mother's womb
 that they enjoy th'embodied state,
And others fuse into a plant,
 as knowledge and their deeds dictate.

—Kaṭha 5.7

51. Attached to this world, one who acts self-seeking
 enjoys the results of his actions later.
He wanders about because of his actions,
 reborn with the gods, the Fathers or elsewhere.[1]

—Svetāś.5.7

52. One God there is hidden in ev'ry creature
 the Self of all creatures, and all-pervading,

---

1. For the sake of the metre triguṇas has been omitted and prāṇādhipah and viśvarūpas-trivartmā have been paraphrased.

Abiding in all, overseer of Karma,
sole Witness, Observer, beyond the Guṇas.

—*Svetāś. 6. 11.*

SALVATION BY GRACE

53. Smaller than the smallest, the great surpassing,
in the heart of creatures the Self is hidden.
One with no desire becomes freed from sorrow,
when by Grace of God he beholds His glory.

—*Svetāś. 3.20.*

PART - III

Non-dualism
or
the Spiritual Life

BRAHMAN

(a) Two Modes

54. Verily there are two modes of Brahman: that with form and the formless, the mortal and the immortal, the fixed and the moving, the actual and the beyond.

—Brhad.2.3.1

55. He desired, Would that I were many; Let me procreate myself. He underwent religious austerity. Having undergone austerity, He projected all this, whatever there is here. Having projected that, He entered into it. Having entered into it, He became the actual and the beyond.

—Taittirīya 2.6

56. Such the Brahman's mighty power,
but greater still the Person here.
Just a quarter is all beings,
quarters three the gods up there.

—Chāndogya 3.12.6

57. Formless is the Person bright,
within and yet outside the soul;
Anterior to both life and mind,
unborn, the Transcendental Goal.[1]

—Muṇḍaka 2.1.2

58. Unmoving, the One than the mind is swifter:
the senses fell back as ahead It speeded.
Though standing, It passes all others running.
The Air by its presence supports the Waters
It moves and yet It does not move;
That One is far and also near;
That is found within all this,
and also outside can appear.

—Īsa. 4-5

59. The eye may try but cannot reach It,
neither speech can reach nor mind;
We do not know how one could teach It
even were It here to find.
From ancient sages we have heard
that from the known It differs quite,

1. Śubhra is not translated and the last two words are a paraphrase.

(This is the way they explained it)
and from th'unknown as day from night.

—Kena 3

60. Neither grasped by sight nor the other senses,
not by speech not penance nor sacrifices,
But made pure by brightness of understanding,
then may one perceive It in meditation.

—Muṇḍaka 3.1.8

(b) Brahman Beyond

61. Now therefore the teaching—Not thus, not thus, for there is no other teaching higher than this, that He is not thus. Now His name is the Real of the real.

—Bṛhad.2.3.6

(c) Brahman Without (Maya)

62. He served as the Pattern for ev'ry creature;
this Cosmos is there for His revelation.
The Lord by his powers appears in many ways;
to tens and to hundreds are yoked His steeds,
the Bays.

—Bṛhad, 2.5.19

63. By the mind it must be known,
no place here for diversity;
Death obtains he after death,
who seeming difference thinks to see.

—Bṛhad. 4.4.19

64. As by a bowl or plate of gold,
the Real's face is hid from me.
O Pūṣan, pray uncover that
for me who speaks the truth to see.

—*Bṛhad.5.15.1.*

65. The hymns, sacrifices, oblations, customs,
the past and the future,. the Vedic teachings
From Brahman the Master projects this world all;
in which t'other Person is bound by Maya.
Know that Nature is illusion,
th'illusion—maker is the Lord;
Full of beings as his members
one may know this world is stored

—*Śvetāśvatara 4. 9-10*

(b) Brahman within *(Puruṣa)*

66. This Being primeval pervades all quarters,
the first to be born, in the womb subsisting
Of old He was born, will be born in future,
indwelling His offspring in ev'ry region.

—*Śvetās 2.16*

67. With eyes and with mouth all directions facing,
with arms and with feet all directions moving,
The one God, producing the earth and heaven,
them welds with His arms and His wings as
bellows.

—*Śvetāś 3.3*

68. The Person has a thousand heads,
a thousand feet, a thousand eyes;
The earth surroundings on all sides,
ten fingers' breadth beyond He lies.

—*Śvetāś, 3. 14*

69. You are man and you are woman,
you the groom and also bride,
Old, you use a stick as guide,
born, you wander having face on ev'ry side.

—*Śvetāś 4.3*

ATMAN

(a) The Inner Controller

70. He entered in here upto the ends of the nails, just as a razor might be placed in a razor-case or fire in a fire-holder. They do not see Him, for He is incomplete: when breathing, He is called the breath; when speaking, the voice; when seeing, the eye; when hearing, thc ear; when thinking, the mind. These are only the names of His actions.

—*Bṛhad. 1.4.7*

71. Then Usasta Cākrāyaṇa asked him: "O Yājnavalkya!" he said. "Explain to me what is the Brahman, immediate and direct, which is the Self wihtin all?"

"It is your Self within all."

"O Yājnavalkya! Which of the Selves is it that is within all?

"It is your Self within all which breathes in by your breathing in...

.... You cannot see the Seer of seeing; you cannot hear the Hearer of hearing; you cannot think the Thinker of thinking; you cannot know the Knower of knowing. That is Your Self within all.

—*Bṛhad.3.4.1-2*

72. Moved by whom does thinking attain its object?
Who directs the function of vital breathing?
Moved by whom do people engage in speaking?
Say what force directs both the sight and hearing,
He, the hearing's Hearer, the thinking's Thinker.
speaking's Speaker, even the breathing's Breather,
Eye of eye. The wise by renouncing find Him;
parting from this world they become immortal.

—*Kena 1-2*

73. That which dwelling within all things is yet other than all things, which all things do not know, whose body is all things, which controls all things from within, He is your own Self, The Inner Controller, the Immortal....

—*Bṛhad.3.7. 23*

74. .... He is the Unseen seer, the Unheard Hearer, The Unthought thinker, The Unknown knower;

there is no other seer than this, there is no other hearer than this, there is no other thinker than this, there is no other knower than this: this is your own Self, the Inner Controller, the Immortal...

—*Bṛhad.3.7. 23*

(b) The Witness

75. Spirit is not born, nor deceases ever,
    has not come from any, nor from it any.
This Unborn, Eternal and Everlasting
    Ancient is not slain, be it slain the body.

—*Kaṭha 2.18*

76. Knowing that great pervasive Self
    as that through which one can perceive
Both states of waking and of sleep,
    the wise man will no longer grieve.

—*Kaṭha 4.4*

(c) The Person the Size of a Thumb

77. The Person of a thumb in size
    within one's very self abides;
The Lord of past and of future,
    from Him, when once he's known, none hides
This verily is That.
This Person of a thumb in size
    is like a light with smokeless ray;
The Lord of past and of future
    exists tomorrow and today.
This verily is That.

—*Kaṭha 4. 12-13*

(d) The Inner Light

78. Yonder Shining Light of lights
Self-knowers see within their hearts,
In a golden sheath on high,
the Brahman, stainless, free from parts.
There no sun is shining, nor moon and stars so bright,
neither shine these lightnings, much less this earthly light
All things wordly shine to reflect His glory:
by His light alone is this world illumined
—Muṇḍaka 2.2. 9-10

BRAHMAN · ATMAN

79. He who consists of the mind, whose body is breath, whose form is the light of Consciousness, whose resolve is true, whose Self is space, containing all actions, containing all desires, containing all odours, containing all taste, pervading this whole world, the unspeaking, the unconcerned; this my Self within the heart is smaller than a grain of rice, or a barely-corn, or a mustard-seed, or a grain of millet, or the kernel of a grain of millet; this my Self within the heart is larger than the earth, larger than the sky, larger than the heavens, larger than all these worlds. *—Chāndogya 3.14. 2-3*

80. "Bring a banyan-fruit from there."
"Here it is, my lord."

"Break it."
"It is broken, my lord."
"What do you see there?"
"These rather fine seeds, my lord."
"Well, break one of them."
"It is broken, my lord."
"What do you see there?"
"Nothing, my lord."

He said to him, "My boy, this finest essence which you do not perceive, verily, my boy, from that finest essence the large banyan thus arises. Believe me, my boy.

That finest essence which the whole world has for its self, that is the True, that is the Self, that you are, O Śvetaketu..."

—Chāndogya 6.12.1-3

THE FOUR MAHAVAKYAS

81. All this is guided by Consciousness, is based on Consciousness... Brahman is Consciousness (PRĀJNANAM BRAHMA)— Aitereya 5.3 (Rigveda). That is the True; That is the Self; That art thou (TAT TVAM ASI).

—Chāndogya 6.8.7 etc. (sāmaveda)

Whoever knows this, "I am Brahman," (AHAM BRAHMĀSMI) becomes this all.

—Brhad.1.4. 10 (Yajurveda)

For truly everything here is Brahman, and this Self also is Brahman (AYAM ATMĀ BRAHMA).

—*Māṇḍūkya 2 (Atharvaveda)*

THE HIGHER ETHICS

82. All living things that are on earth
 must be enveloped by the Self.
You may enjoy what is renounced,
 so covet not another's pelf.
But even as a worker one
 may wish to live a hundred year,
To you if such a man - not other -
 wise - the deed will not adhere.

—*Īśa 1-2*

83. He who sees the core of ev'ry
 being in himself alone,
And his Self in ev'ry being,
 to dislike is never prone.
When all beings have become
 the very self of such a seer,
What delusion or what sorrow,
 seeing oneness ev'rywhere?

—*Īsa 6-7*

84. There are three branches of religous duty: i. sacrifice, study of the Vedas, and alms-giving are the first; ii. severe meditation alone is ths second; iii. a student of the Vedas dwelling in the home of

1. Interpreted according to Brahma Sutras 3.4.19.

the teacher (exhausting himself exceedingly in the home of the teacher) is the third. All these become possessors of meritorious worlds. iv. He who is wholly devoted to Brahman attains immortality.[1]

—*Chāndogya 2.23.1*

THREE NEEDS

(a) For Realisation

85. Yājnavalkya said: "Lo! The husband verily is dear not out of love for the husband, but the husband is dear out of love for the Self. Lo! The wife verily is dear not out of love for the wife, but the wife is dear out of love for the Self. Lo! Sons verily are dear not out of love for sons, but sons are dear out of love for the Self Lo! All things verily are dear not out of love for all things, but all things are dear out of love for the Self. Lo! The Self verily should be realised: should be heared, should be reflected on, should be meditated on, Maitreyi. Lo! Verily everything here is known by the realisation of the Self: through hearing, through reflection, through meditation.

—*Bṛhad. 2.4.5*

86. Religious mendicants wander forth from their homes seeking this same world of the Self alone. For verily the Ancients knowing this did not desire progeny, saying, "What shall we, who have

this Self, this world, do with progeny?" Verily they turned away from the desire for sons, the desire for wealth, and the desire for heaven, and lived the life of mendicancy; for the desire for sons is the desire for wealth, and the desire for wealth is the desire for heaven; both of these are desires.

—*Bṛhad. 4.4.22*

87. His father said to him: "O Śvetaketu, my dear! Since you are haughty and puffed up, regarding yourself as well-versed in the Vedas, did you ask for that instruction by which the Unheard becomes heard, the Unthought - of becomes thought of, the Ununderstood becomes understood?" "Of what nature indeed is that instruction, sir?"

"My dear, just as through a single lump of clay everything made of clay would be understood, for the modification is but a name depending on mere words, and the clay alone is real, so, my dear, is that instruction."

—*Chāndogya 6.1.2-4*

88. My dear, just as one might lead away a man from the land of the Gandhāras with his eyes blindfolded and leave him in an uninhabited place, and just as there he might cryout to the east or to the north or to the south or to the west that he had been led away blindfolded and left; just as if someone, after removing his blindfold, might say, "The Land of the Gandhāras is in that direction; go in

that direction;" and asking his way from village to village and being informed, he would, if he were an intelligent man, arrive at the same land of the Gandhāras; even so in this world one who has a preceptor knows that only so long is the delay for him as he is not liberated from bondage, then he will be absorbed into Being.

—*Chāndogya 6.14.1-2*

89. By most unobtainable e'en to hear of,
and many though hearing unable to know him.
Amazing the knower taught by the clever-
amazing the teacher, clever the pupil!-

—*Kaṭha 2.7*

90. But he who has no understanding,
aye unmindful, full of stains,
Never reaches that abode,
only repeated birth obtains.
But he who is with understanding,
ever mindful, free from stain,
Verily reaches that abode
from which he is not born again.

—*Katha 3.7-8*

(b) For a Guru

91. If by an inferior man instructed
unknown is the Reai, though often pondered,
No access unless It is taught by a better,
because inconceivably subtler than subtlest.

—*Kaṭha 2.8*

92. Arise! Awake! 'Tis time to turn
And seek the first-rate ones and learn.
The sages declare that path hard to tread on-
Impassable like the sharp edge of razor.-

—Kaṭha 3.14

93. These matters manifest become
to that great soul, when they are taught,
Who for the Lord shows great devotion,
and for the Guru as for Lord

—Śvetāśvatara 4.23

(c) For Grace

94. This Self is not knowable by instruction,
nor by mental power, nor by much learning;
Alone is It known by the one It chooses:
this Self of Itself then reveals Its nature.

—Muṇḍaka 3.2.3

95. The Pilgrim is whirled round in Brahman's
Tread-wheel,
in which live and die all creatures whatever.
But seeing himself as the motive power,
thereby he is blest and gains life immortal.

—Śvetāśvatara 1.6

DESCRIPTION OF THE TRANCE STATE

96. When everything has become the very Self, then what should one see and through what? Then what should one smell and through what? Then

what should one taste and through what? Then what should one speak and through what? Then what should one hear and through what? Then what should one think and through what? Then what should one touch and through what? Then what should one know and through what?
Through what should one know that by means of which one knows all this?...

—*Bṛhad. 6.5.15*

97. Not inwardly cognitive, nor outwardly cognitive, nor both-wise cognitive; not an indefinite mass of congntion, not collective congnition, not non-cognition. It is unseen, unrelated, imperceptible, indefinable, inconceivable, indescribable. It is the essence of the one self-cognition common to all states of consciousness. All phenomena cease in it. It is tranquil, beneficent, free from duality—such they consider the Fourth; that is the Self, that is to be realised. —*Māṇḍūkya 7*

98. For where there is duality, as it were, then one smells another, then one sees another, then one hears another, then one addresses another, then one thinks of another, then one knows another; but where all has become the very Self of the Knower of Brahman, whom and through what would one smell, then whom and through what would one see, then whom and through what would one hear, then whom and through what would one address, then of whom and through what

would one think, then whom and through what would one think, then whom and through what would one know? Through what would one know That through which one knows everything here? Lo! Through what would one know the knower?

—Bṛhad. 2.4.14

99. Verily that which is Infinite[1] is happiness; there is no happiness in the finite; the Infinite alone is happiness....

Where one sees nothing else, hears nothing else, understands nothing else, that is the Infinite; but where one sees something else, hears something else, understands something else, that is the finite. Verily that which is the Infinite is alone immortal, but that which is finite is mortal....

—Chāndogya 7.23-26

LIBERATION

100. Now he who does not desire—who is without desire, who is freed from desire, whose desires have been fulfilled, whose desire is for the Self only—his energies do not pass away; being the very Brahman he goes to Brahman.

Therefore there is this verse;

"When are given up all longings
which are found in heart and soul,
Then the mortal becomes immortal,
in this life attains the Goal."

Then just as the slough of a snake might lie on ananthill, lifeless and cast off, even so this body lies, and this incorporeal immortal life-force is Brahman Itself, the Light Itself...

There are these verses:

"That difficult path, but diffused and ancient,
by me has been reached and by me discovered.
Wise knowers of Brahman, released hereafter,
by this path enter the highest heaven.

—Bṛhad 4.4 6-8

101. Those who know the meaning of Vedic doctrines,
holy men made pure by renunciation,
Past the fear of dying are liberated
in the highest heaven, when falls the body.

—Muṇḍaka 3.2.6

102. He who indeed knows that Brahman Supreme, becomes very Brahman; none ignorant of Brahman is born in his family.
He crosses o'er sorrow, he crosses o'er sin,
from the knots of the heart liberated, he becomes immortal.[1]

—Muṇḍaka 3.2.9

103. God has bored the opening outward-facing,
thus one sees the outer but not the inner:
Some wise man desiring the life eternal
inwards turned his sight and beheld his Spirit.

—Kaṭha 4.1

---

1. In the text this looks like poetry, but reads as prose.

104. As pure water becomes the same
when into water pure it flows,
So of the sage, O Gautama,
the Self becomes who Brahman knows.

—*Kaṭha 4. 15*

105. The Self of all creatures, the One Controller,
who makes his one form into many objects,
Is seen by the wise to exist inside them;
such men and no others have Bliss Eternal.

—*Kaṭha 5. 12*

106. His form isn't set up where one can see it;
no one can perceive that One through the senses.
But He is revealed by the understanding
and feelings. Who knows this become immortal.

—*Kaṭha 4. 9*

107. Ghora Angirasa, addressing Krishna, son of Devaki, said this (he had become free from desire), "At the time of death one should resort to this triad: You are the Indestructibe; You are the Imperishable; You are animated by the Vital Airs."

In this connection there are two Riks:
"Then from its ancient source indeed
(the Light they see at early morn,
Kindled beyond the heaven's bourn.)"
"Gazing up out of the darkness

to scrutinise the higher Light,
to scrutinise the higher Light,
The Sun, a god among the gods,
we now have reached the Highest Light,
tho Highest Light"

—Chāndogya 3.17.6-7

108. I know, I speak truly, this mighty Person
as bright as the sun, and beyond the
darkness.
Whoever has seen Him deceases never-
no other procedure for thus escaping.-

—Śvetaś.3.8

Index